OCTOPUS VS. SPINY LOBSTER

BY NATHAN SOMMER

BELLWETHER MEDIA • MINNEAPOLIS, MN

Torque brims with excitement
perfect for thrill-seekers of all kinds.
Discover daring survival skills, explore
uncharted worlds, and marvel at mighty
engines and extreme sports. In *Torque* books,
anything can happen. Are you ready?

This edition first published in 2025 by Bellwether Media, Inc.

No part of this publication may be reproduced in whole or in part without
written permission of the publisher.
For information regarding permission, write to Bellwether Media, Inc.,
Attention: Permissions Department,
6012 Blue Circle Drive, Minnetonka, MN 55343.

Library of Congress Cataloging-in-Publication Data

LC record for Octopus vs. Spiny Lobster available at:
https://lccn.loc.gov/2024019761

Editor: Suzane Nguyen   Designer: Hunter Demmin

Printed in the United States of America, North Mankato, MN.

TABLE OF CONTENTS

THE COMPETITORS

The world's **tropical** oceans are home to many animals. Octopuses use their arms and beaks to hunt for **prey** on the ocean floor.

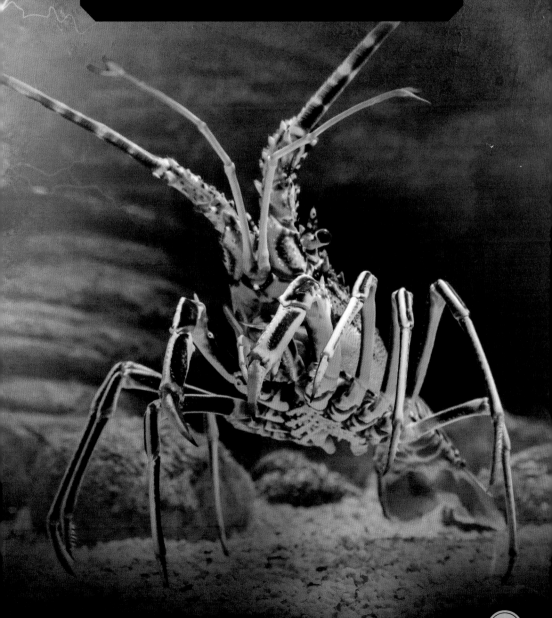

Octopuses share this **habitat** with spiny lobsters. These **crustaceans** have sharp, spiky bodies that keep them safe. But who really rules the ocean floor?

Octopuses have rounded bodies, large eyes, and eight long arms. Their arms have two rows of powerful suckers. They use these to **grip**, smell, and taste.

There are about 300 types of octopuses. The biggest grow up to 16 feet (4.9 meters) long. Octopuses are found in every ocean. Many live along the ocean floor.

COMMON OCTOPUS

DEN DWELLERS

Many octopuses live in hidden holes and cracks in rocks.

COMMON OCTOPUS PROFILE

0   2 FEET   4 FEET

LENGTH
AROUND 4.3 FEET
(1.3 METERS)

WEIGHT
UP TO 22 POUNDS
(10 KILOGRAMS)

HABITAT

OCEANS

COMMON OCTOPUS RANGE

☐ RANGE

CARIBBEAN SPINY LOBSTER PROFILE

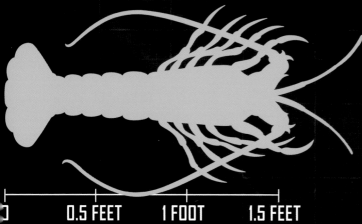

```
           0.5 FEET      1 FOOT      1.5 FEET
```

LENGTH
UP TO 1.5 FEET
(0.5 METERS)

WEIGHT
UP TO 15 POUNDS
(6.8 KILOGRAMS)

HABITAT

TROPICAL OCEANS

CARIBBEAN SPINY LOBSTER RANGE

■ RANGE

Spiny lobsters weigh up to 15 pounds (6.8 kilograms). They can grow up to 1.5 feet (0.5 meters) long. The lobsters have pointed spines, reddish-brown shells, and hornlike **antennae**.

Spiny lobsters live in tropical oceans. Many live within seagrass, rocky **reefs**, and cracks along the ocean floor.

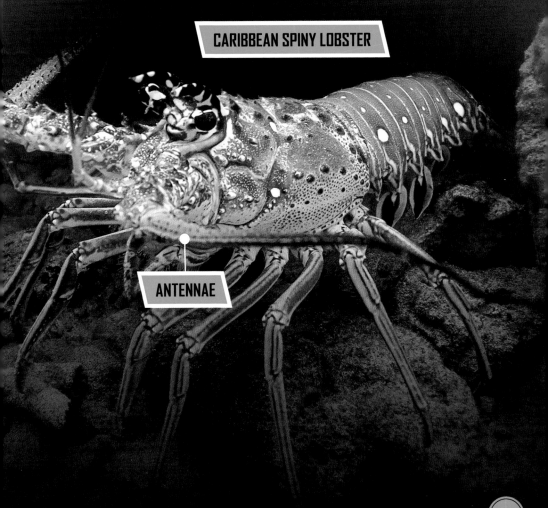

CARIBBEAN SPINY LOBSTER

ANTENNAE

SECRET WEAPONS

Special body parts help octopuses change colors fast. The animals easily change to match nearby surroundings. Octopuses instantly **camouflage** before **predators** can see them!

LOBSTER SIZE

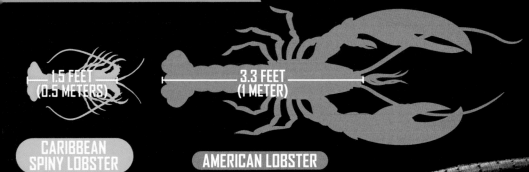

1.5 FEET (0.5 METERS)

3.3 FEET (1 METER)

CARIBBEAN SPINY LOBSTER

AMERICAN LOBSTER

Spiny lobsters do not have claws. Sharp, forward pointing spines protect them. These stab enemies who try to grab the lobsters. The spines prevent the lobsters from being eaten.

ARM LENGTH

3 FEET (0.9 METERS)	2.5 FEET (0.8 METERS)
COMMON OCTOPUS	HUMAN MALE

Some octopuses use their sucker-covered arms to easily capture prey. They wrap their long arms around animals. Prey cannot escape!

Spiny lobsters have **antennules**. These special parts can smell for food and nearby predators. The antennules help the lobsters hunt and hide from enemies.

ANTENNULES

SHEDDED SHELLS

Spiny lobsters shed their shells to grow. They do this around 25 times before they reach adulthood.

SECRET WEAPONS

CAMOUFLAGE

POWERFUL ARMS

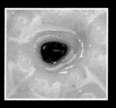

SHARP BEAK

BEAK

Octopuses have sharp beaks. They use their beaks to break the hard shells of prey. Their bites also **inject** prey with **venom**. This stops prey from moving.

SECRET WEAPONS

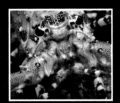

SHARP SPINES

ANTENNULES

LONG ANTENNAE

Spiny lobsters use their hornlike antennae to protect themselves. They wave their antennae to warn enemies to stay away. If this does not work, they use the sharp antennae to fight!

ATTACK MOVES

A TIGHT SQUEEZE

Beaks are the only hard part on octopuses' bodies. They can squeeze into any place bigger than their beaks!

Octopuses often **ambush** prey from above. They remain hidden until the perfect moment. They catch prey using their powerful arms. Then, they push their meals toward their sharp beaks.

Spiny lobsters are **opportunistic** hunters. They use spiky front legs to hunt. The lobsters eat crabs, shrimp, and **carrion** along the ocean floor.

Octopuses shoot out ink when in danger. This blocks predators from seeing or smelling them. Octopuses quickly escape by sucking water into their bodies and shooting it back out.

ENDLESS ARMS

Octopus arms grow back after being removed or cut off.

Spiny lobsters flick their tails to quickly escape danger. They jab enemies with their long, sharp antennae when cornered. If predators catch them, many find the lobsters' spiny bodies too hard to eat.

READY,
FIGHT!

A hidden octopus follows a spiny lobster. The lobster senses the octopus's movements. The lobster flicks its tail to escape. But the octopus quickly grabs the lobster with its arms.

The lobster stabs the octopus with its sharp antennae. This hurts the octopus. The lobster hides in a crack as the hurt octopus swims away. The lobster avoids being eaten today!

GLOSSARY

ambush—to carry out a surprise attack

antennae—long, thin body parts on the heads of lobsters

antennules—thin parts on lobsters' heads that help lobsters smell things

camouflage—to use colors and patterns to help an animal hide in its surroundings

carrion—the remains of a dead animal

crustaceans—animals that have several pairs of legs and hard outer shells; lobsters and crabs are types of crustaceans.

grip—to tightly hold

habitat—a home or area where an animal prefers to live

inject—to force a fluid into something

opportunistic—taking advantage of a situation

predators—animals that hunt other animals for food

prey—animals that are hunted by other animals for food

reefs—underwater structures formed by rocks or coral

tropical—having to do with a place that is hot and wet

venom—a kind of poison used to hurt or paralyze enemies

TO LEARN MORE

AT THE LIBRARY

Clarke, Ginjer L. *Octopus!: Smartest in the Sea?*. New York, N.Y.: Penguin Young Readers, 2024.

Culliford, Amy. *Ocean Animal Habitats*. New York, N.Y.: Crabtree Publishing, 2024.

Spencer, Erin. *The Incredible Octopus: Meet the Eight-armed Wonder of the Sea*. North Adams, Mass.: Storey Publishing, 2024.

ON THE WEB

FACTSURFER

Factsurfer.com gives you a safe, fun way to find more information.

1. Go to www.factsurfer.com

2. Enter "octopus vs. spiny lobster" into the search box and click 🔍.

3. Select your book cover to see a list of related web sites.

INDEX

The images in this book are reproduced through the courtesy of: Olga Visavi, front cover (octopus); imageBROKER.com GmbH & Co. KG, front cover (spiny lobster); Brenda Borgo, pp. 2-3, 19, 20-24; Rich Carey, pp. 2-3, 20-24; Sakis Lazarides, p. 4; Gilmanshin, p. 5; Henner Damke, pp. 6-7; MYP Studio, pp. 8-9; Richard Whitcombe, pp. 10, 14 (camouflage); Ethan Drake, pp. 11, 15 (main, antennules, long antennae);Kondratuk Aleksei, p. 12; bcampbell65, p. 13; The Picture Pantry Ltd. / Alamy StockPhoto/ Alamy, p. 14 (main); N Kotek, p. 14 (powerful arms); lay london, p. 14 (sharp beak); Vladimir Wrangel, p. 15 (sharp spines); Divelvanov, p. 16; Becky Gill, p. 17; Vittorio Bruno, p. 18.